MW00886526

This Book Belongs To:

____

Made in the USA
Monee, IL
13 March 2021

62627138R00056